wee words fo

prese

10•10 Poetry
Anthology

Celebrating 10
in 10 Different Ways

edited and compiled by

Bridget Magee

This book is dedicated to all of my loves:
Joe, Co, and Mo (and Smidgey-oh!)

Copyright ©2021, Bridget Magee. All Rights Reserved.
ISBN: 978-1-7373303-0-1

wee words for wee ones
Hünenberg See CH

www.bridgetmagee.com

Table of Contents

Dear Reader   **8**

Tentative   **10**

"Necessary In-tent" by Mary E. Cronin

"Electric" by Tabatha Yeatts

"Step Into the Unknown" by Jennifer Raudenbush

"Stray" by Michelle Heidenrich Barnes

"Hand in Hand" by Christy Mihaly

"Am I Tentative? A Poem in Two Voices" by Karen Eastlund

"Tentatively Certain..." by Michelle Kogan

haiku by Linda J. Thomas

"Pond•ering" by Christy Mihaly

Tenderness   **18**

"Blue" by Eileen Spinelli

"A Hand to Hold" by Kay Jernigan McGriff

"Tend Her, Breeze" by Donna JT Smith

"Do Not Lose Your Song" by Alan j Wright

"Trees" by Jennifer Raudenbush

"Moon" by Eileen Spinelli

"The Two of Us" by Alan j Wright

"In the Brambles" by Lisa Varchol Perron

"Entwined" by Molly Hogan

"Cat Nap" by Daniel J. Flore III

Tenacity   **28**

"Dear Tooth Fairy" by Laura Shovan

"Not This Time" by Elisabeth Norton

haiku by Mary Lee Hahn

"I Carry On" by Corinne Hertel

"You've Gotta Keep Searching" by Alan j Wright

"The Crow" by Geraldine Tyler

"Usain" by Kathleen Mazurowski

"Tenacious Place Holder" by Linda J. Thomas

"My Baby Brother" by Carmelo A. Martino

"Tough Guy" by Lisa Varchol Perron

Ten More Minutes   **39**

"Mama, Can You Spare Some Time?" by Colleen Owen Murphy

"The Alarm Went Off" by Janet Wong

"Ten More Minutes...A Matter of Perspective" by Jay Brazeau

"Wake Up!" by Meenakshi Dwivedi

"Time to Leave the Beach Playground" by Carmela A. Martino

"Mud Pies & Manatees" by Aixa Perez-Prado

"Extra Needed" by Linda Baie

"I Couldn't Put It Down" by Alan j Wright

Tension   **47**

"The Greatest Show on Earth" by Marilyn Garcia

"The Floating Water Strider" by Janice Scully

"Counting Down..." by David Edge

"Her Fur Is Soft as Mittens, But..." by Laura Purdie Salas

"Why Raindrops Are Round" by Janice Scully

"The Grammar Police" by Alan j Wright

"Releasing the Tension" by Carmela A. Martino

"Tug of War" by Moe Phillips

"His Chair" by Angela De Groot

I Wouldn't Touch That with a **Ten** Foot Pole **60**

"Crocodile" by Meenakshi Dwivedi

"I Wouldn't Touch That With A Ten-Foot Pole" by Mary Lee Hahn

"10 Things I Wouldn't Do" by Elizabeth Steinglass

"At Your Disposal" by Colleen Owen Murphy

"A Smoother Frog" by Kay Jernigan McGriff

"Old King Cole's Secret" by Stephan Stuecklin

"Mud Café" by Jennifer Raudenbush

"I Would Not or Maybe I Would" by Kathleen Mazurowski

"Reverie Diary" by Tabatha Yeatts

Ten Little Fingers/Ten Little Toes   **70**

"Finger Counting Rhyme" by Linda Mitchell

haiku by David Edge

"Tenderness Times Ten" by Susan Bruck

"Ten Little Fingers" by Elenore Byrne

"Otter" by Buffy Silverman

"Ten Fingers, One Piano" by Susan Johnston Taylor

"To Ten...And Then Again" by Dave Goodale

"Hand Prints" by Kelly Conroy

"Celebrating Baby's Digits" by Carol Varsalona

Take Ten   **78**

"Kitchen Band" by Cathy Chester

"Keeping the Peace" by Angela De Groot

"Respite" by Helen Magee

"Take 10 to Find Ten" by Janet Fagal

"Counting on Mistakes" by Kay Jernigan McGriff

"Sea Glass Searching" by Shannah Salter

"Ten Ghosts" by Meenakshi Dwivedi

Tenth _____ **87**

"My Tenth Birthday" by Eileen Spinelli

"Tenth of an Inch" by Maureen Magee-Uhlik

"Winning at Tenth" by Karen Edmisten

"Tenth Month" by Irene Latham

"the amber light of the sun" by Linda M. Crate

"Tenth Text Says It All" by Ruth Hersey

"The Jaunty Letter J" by Bridget Magee

I **Ten**d To... **97**

"Tend With Wonder" by Marty Lapointe-Malchik

"TLC" by Robyn Hood Black

"A Professional Riddle" by Elisabeth Norton

"Quitting" by Rebekah Hoeft

"Weathered Tendencies" by Linda Baie

"Talking to Hear Myself Speak" by Bridget Magee

"through the years" by Linda M. Crate

"I'm Sorry" by Linda Kulp Trout

"What Tends to Happen" by Karen Eastlund

Who Wrote What **106**

Dear Reader,

On New Year's Eve 2020 I made the **TENATIVE** decision to compile and edit a poetry anthology to celebrate the 10th Anniversary of wee words for wee ones.

As the **TENTH** child born into a family of *ten* children in the *tenth* month, I am forever fascinated by the number *ten*. Add **TENACITY** to that fascination and the idea to create this anthology was conceived.

I TEND TO jump into projects with a pure heart, but a murky understanding of the logistics. This project was no different.

I can honestly say I have a newfound **TENDERNESS** for editors. (Understatement.)

As submissions poured in from around the world, I had a fair amount of **TENSION** knowing I had to reject many, many high-quality poems because they didn't fit the overall theme or 10 categories. So many times, I wanted to **TAKE TEN** more poems (plus ten!) than I could. A very good problem to have.

I was recently asked, "Which poem in the anthology is your favorite?" Now that's a question **I WOULDN'T TOUCH WITH A TEN FOOT POLE!** But I can say I am eternally grateful to every one of the poets featured in this book, both new and established, whose work literally made this anthology possible.

Along with my gratitude I need to apologize as well. To my biggest cheerleader, my husband, Joe, I am sorry for always calling out, **"TEN MORE MINUTES"** when working on this anthology. Time is fleeting when you are tending to a labor of love. (See what I did there?)

Just like a mamma or daddy who counts **TEN LITTLE FINGERS** and **TEN LITTLE TOES** as they welcome their new creation into the world, I present to you the ***10 •10 Poetry Anthology: Celebrating 10 in 10 Different Ways***.

Ten months to curate, a lifetime to enjoy.

♡,

Bridget

"Every step, even a **tentative** *one, counts."*

~ Anne Morrow Lindbergh

Necessary In-tent

Deep in the woods, I'm in a small tent--

a camping trip—why did I say *yes*?

The nighttime woods are dark and dense,

full of snapping twigs, strange scents.

It's just twenty steps to the "rest room,"

but there is no rest.

Twenty steps I need to take— I'm stressed!

In the woods there's no such thing as a fence,

no defense against bears, snakes,

insects.

Branches throw shadows, gnarled and bent,

as I unzip my tent.

I take a deep breath,

   I stick out a toe—

      here I go.

~Mary E. Cronin

Electric

There once was a young man so shy,

he never looked girls in the eye.

He mastered guitar

and became a star –

how his confidence did amplify!

~ Tabatha Yeatts

Step Into the Unknown

So much depends upon a chance Kool-Aid mustache

in deciding to step into the neighbor's yard

—and into friendship.

~Jennifer Raudenbush

Stray

A balmy morning, rain
hung like a pregnant
pause, you brushed against
the dumpster, claiming
it as your own, while I,
like a lonely hydrant, sat
watching from the curb,
hoping for a furry flank,
a tail around my leg, wishing
to be claimed by a stray
ginger tabby. For one timeless
moment your golden eyes
met mine, so I offered my palm—
and then you were gone,
danger crashing
around you like thunder
and lightning, and I
plodded home in the rain.

~ Michelle Heidenrich Barnes

Hand in Hand

Grampa walks me home from practice.

Luckily, I know the way.

Every time, he asks, "Which corner?"

So I show him:

  "Here!" I say.

~ Christy Mihaly

Am I Tentative? A Poem for Two Voices

1: People say I'm tentative

          2: Are you?

1: Beats me...

          2: What does tentative mean?

1: Your guess is as good as mine

          2: Is it a bad thing?

1: I'm not sure

          2: Will you find out?

1: Probably

          2: Will you let me know?

1: It's possible

          2: But...will you?

1: I'll consider it

          2: Do you think it is contagious?

1: It could be

          2: How dangerous is it?

1: I can only guess

          2: Are you always so iffy?

1: You might say so

2: This conversation is so frustrating I could scream

1: Maybe I'll join you

2: AAAaaauugghhh!!!!

~ Karen Eastlund

Tentatively Certain...

I hate to be tentative, usually I'm not,
But lately my mind's filled with unsettled thought...

I go to bed early but can't settle down
I wake up all groggy–and feel so rundown.

I move through my zombie-womby like day
As if by the end I'll see clear as a jay.

If my friends ask me questions, I hem and I haw...
I hesitate till they finally withdraw.

But please don't give up on me, hear my new theory–
Be patient, it's short and won't make you weary...

I'll read–and read–and read some more
Till I dream of certainty, and things that are sure...

I think it'll work.
I think I should try.
I think my idea will take off and fly.

~ *Michelle Kogan*

One paw print outside

in the snow on our front step;

our cat still inside.

~ *Linda J. Thomas*

16

Pond·ering

This pond, I fear, is freezing cold.

The murky water's much too deep;

the slimy shore is much too steep.

There's *water wolves* down there, I'm told,

and eww, that green stuff looks like mold.

Is that a log? Or did it blink?

And what is that peculiar stink?

You're jumping in? Not me, no way!

Wait! "Marco Polo"? Let me play!

This pond is really nice, I think.

~ *Christy Mihaly*

*"The quality of strength lined with **tenderness** is an unbeatable combination..."*

~ Maya Angelou

Blue

Blue by blue
the sky unfolds
almost like a flower.
Flower-scent flutters down.
Our hands are warm
with petals.
We sing this tender unfolding
of sky
to one another across
fields...fences...back alleys...
We call this song
Spring.

~ Eileen Spinelli

A Hand to Hold

When you have a hand to hold,

your fear begins to slip away.

Then your heart can grow so bold

when you have a hand to hold.

No more alone amid the cold,

two clasped hands are here to stay

when you have a hand to hold.

Now fear begins to slip away.

~ Kay Jernigan McGriff

Tend Her, Breeze

                    breeze,

                 flow, hum,

              swirl her hair

            in sweet ringlets,

         tenderly d r i f t her

          giggles and laughter

         in cloud brushed sky

            through the air,

               blow, strum,

                  breeze

               ~ Donna JT Smith

Do Not Lose Your Song

When the sorrows of the wider world

pile up at your door

Do not lose your song

Every bird in the forest

contributes to the morning chorus

Do not lose your song.

            ~ Alan j Wright

Trees

The porch swing rocks—
now front, now back.
Its rhythmic song—
now click, now clack.

My breathing slows—
flows out, flows in,
a bow across
a violin.

I notice singing
from the trees.
Leaves sigh and rustle
in the breeze.

No longer is it
them and me,
For now we sway
in harmony.

And I am one
with wind, with tree;
we dance as one
in unity.

~ Jennifer Raudenbush

Moon

I am the moon, child,
mothering you from afar.

In tenderness
my light falls across
your darkest dreams...
shows them to be simply
stage paint and pins.

Sleep, child,
softly,
safely,
in the long, lingering light of
your mothermoon.

~ Eileen Spinelli

The Two of Us

If you were a fish
I'd be a frog
I'd watch you swim by
While I sat on a log

If you were a cupcake
I'd be your icing
I would try very hard
To protect you from slicing

If you were a kite
I'd be your string
We'd dance in the sky
High above everything

I just want to tell you
You're special my friend
Through good time and bad
I'm with you 'til the end.

~ Alan j Wright

In the Brambles

I pick blackberries
until my scraped skin stings.
Raw red
against
the deep purple harvest.

My cousin calls me tender.
Hands unworn,
uncalloused,
untested—
much like my heart.

The jab
prickles,
but I know—
her thorns
provide protection,
guard against intruders
who swoop in
and steal her berries.

Then she smiles,
softens,
shows me how
to reach between the brambles
and find fruit
ready for plucking.

By summer's end
my skin will toughen,
but like my cousin,

I'll stay tender
on the inside.

~ Lisa Varchol Perron

Entwined

In the flush
of our adolescent courtship
we always held hands,
fingers knit together
skin against skin.

In our private language
each movement
held meaning.
We could whisper
"I love you"
with the brush
of a pinky.

Decades later,
recalling
the exquisite sensitivity
of my palm
awaiting your gentle stroke,
our laced fingers
as intimate
as private
as limbs intertwined...
I blush.   ~ *Molly Hogan*

Cat Nap

a cat sleeping
on still warm towels
from the dryer-

dreams of the snowflakes
blowing around outside

-paws at them in her slumber

~ Daniel J. Flore III

*"The most difficult thing is the decision to act, the rest is merely **tenacity**."*

~ Amelia Earhart

Dear Tooth Fairy

You're probably looking
for a tooth under this pillow,
rummaging around
with delicate fairy fingers,
trying not to wake me up.
(Don't worry. Mom says
I sleep like a rock,
but as far as I can tell
rocks don't sleep,
so you can ignore
my mother on this point.)
Mom said you would not
leave me money unless
there was a big fat molar
nestled under my pillow,
waiting to be scooped up
and put in your fairy basket.
(How does she know
it's a basket? Maybe
you carry a backpack
made of dogwood petals.
Pink ones. I'm guessing
you like pink.)

I happen to have a big fat molar.
Or—had one until this morning
during the spelling test
when I chewed my pencil so hard
trying to remember how to spell
"tenacity" that the tooth
which was loose for a week

finally popped out,
skidded across my desk and landed
on Melinda's test paper.
Melinda screamed even though
there wasn't any blood
on the tooth. Not much, anyway.
It was the funniest thing
that has happened so far
in fifth grade, and I'd really
like to remember Melinda's
face and the way she pushed
away from her desk so fast
(to avoid my not-that-bloody
tooth) that she bumped into Henry,
who fell out of his chair.

Tooth Fairy, how will I remember
this moment of epic hilarity
unless I keep my tooth?
Did I mention it's the first
molar I have lost in my whole
10-year-old career of growing
and losing teeth? You, Tooth Fairy,
are a fan of teeth. You get it.
I want to keep this one molar.
I have the perfect place for it,
a birch bark box, small enough
to fit in my hand. (You
probably could fit inside this box.
It would make a nice hangout.
Not that I'm trying to trap you,
or anything. Fly free, Tooth Fairy!)

Do we have a deal? I get to keep
the tooth, you get to laugh
about Melinda's freak out
and Henry falling out of his chair
in the middle of a test. Don't forget
to leave something (a coin or three
would be appreciated,
silver dollars are my favorite
form of currency), that way,
I'll know you were here.

                              ~ *Laura Shovan*

Not This Time

"Fall down seven times, get up eight." — Japanese
Proverb

Ninth time falling,
landing hard,
breath knocked out of me.

Some people stay here
after a fall.
For a while.
Forever.

I could stay here, too.
For a while.
Forever.

I could.

But ...

Tenth time rising,
breathing hard,
dreams not knocked out of me.

Not this time.

                    ~ Elisabeth Norton

green expanse of lawn

trimmed and mowed and manicured

one dandelion

~ *Mary Lee Hahn*

I Carry On

Along the road
Around the lake
Over the mountain
these steps I take.

Never giving up
Brave steps forward
My soul directs
Urging me onward.

Shimmering light
Inspiration real
I carry on stoically
With renewed zeal.

~ *Corinne Hertel*

You've Gotta Keep Searching

I found the missing jigsaw piece

Underneath the rug

I found my missing sock

Stashed in a kitchen jug

I found my old black raincoat

About four years too late

I found the key that went astray

The one that unlocks the front gate

I found my reading glasses

Underneath the bed

I found an autumn leaf

Which had changed from green to red

I found the perfect word to complete a rhyme

And I found the hour I needed

When I was pushed for time

I found a block of chocolate underneath my pillow

And I found my flyaway kite hanging in a weeping

willow.

But, just like Bono

I still haven't found what I'm looking for...

~ Alan j Wright

The Crow

The other day, a cawing crow,
A big black crow
With feathers sleek and shiny beak,
Sat on my fence, all mild and meek.
I didn't mind to have him near
He'd eat some bugs then disappear.

Then, suddenly, an awful shriek
And, swooping down from out the east,
Two tiny birds not breaking stride,
Attacked the crow, from either side.

Swooping and shrieking
They strafed the crow
Who ducked and hopped,
But would not go.

Still, those tiny birds
Just seemed to know
That they could roust Goliath crow
And they persisted in their quest
To defend their nearby nest.
Until that crow did acquiesce
And, cawing, complaining
Flapped off to the west.

And, from that scene, I did recall
Times in my life, both big and small
When I, just like that stubborn crow
Had stayed – long past the time to go.

~ Geraldine Tyler

Usain

There was a kid with capacity

Who had the bold audacity

His goal was to go flying

He didn't give up trying

He sure had a lot of tenacity.

~ *Kathleen Mazurowski*

Tenacious Place Holder

Ten is determined
to be tenth in line,
before eleven and
after nine.

Ten holds on firmly
to its place in line.
Nine to zero MUST
stay behind!

~ *Linda J. Thomas*

My Baby Brother

Wibble, wobble, *step. . . step . . . plop!*
Ben's diaper padding breaks his fall.
He climbs back up, not scared at all.

Wibble, wobble, *step . . . step . . . step . . . thunk!*
Ben's giggling now. He's having fun.
He stands again – all set to run.

Wibble, wobble, *step . . . step . . . step . . . step . . . step . .*
.

Ben grabs my hands. I yell, "Yippee!"
      Dad says, "He's got **tenacity**."
         ~ *Carmela A. Martino*

Tough Guy

You think you rule this kingdom? Wrong!
I'm tiny but I'm tough.
Tenacity's my middle name.
I'm made of stubborn stuff.

Starve me, drown me. I'm still here.
My family tree is growing.
I lost my head three days ago...
So what? I keep on going!

My ancestors were sturdy, too—
surviving mass extinction!
I've earned the right to boast about
this durable distinction.

I'd dare you to debate me, but
you freeze as I approach.
I'm rough and tumble, none too humble.
Call me Cocky Roach!

~ Lisa Varchol Perron

"I have a life expectancy of **ten more minutes** *I'm going to eat what I want to eat."*

~Larry Kramer

Mama, Can You Spare Some Time?

Mama hollers, "Give me ten."
I hate to hear those words again.
'Cause ten turns into minutes more
until she's running out the door,
without a second spent with me,
except a hug (no guarantee).

I get she's got a lot to do
with work and all--it's just us two,
But yesterday I picked a fight;
I need to hear my choice was right.
And so, before this day is done
I'm asking, "Mama, give me one."

~ *Colleen Owen Murphy*

The Alarm Went Off

The alarm went off
in the middle of my dream

I was swimming
in the middle of a scene

swimming like a swordfish
when a shark attacked

and the alarm went off
and I felt heat in my eyes

with one more minute
I would've stabbed its heart

with ten more minutes
I would've been queen of the sea

~ Janet Wong

Ten More Minutes...A Matter of Perspective

on a roller coaster

        with your hand in the

toaster

at a puppy parade

        being afraid

playing pretend

        waiting for a friend

to stay awake

        with a rattlesnake

in your favorite chair

        getting mauled by a bear

as a marshmallow toaster

        on a rollercoaster

Ten more minutes:

    look at it go!   Ten more minutes:

                    (sometimes it's slow).

                    ~ Jay Brazeau

Wake Up!

I hate to leave my cozy bed,
on hearing my mum shout -
I curl into a ball instead,
want to stay inside - not out.

She yells again to see if I'm up.
I know she's reaching her limits.
Diving further into my soft, lovely bed
I reply, "ten more minutes"!

~ *Meenakshi Dwivedi*

Time to Leave the Beach Playground

Just

ten more

minutes? Let

me zoom down the

slide one last time, climb

the monkey bars like a

baby baboon, build a grand

sandcastle with a thousand rooms,

blast off from the swings and cruise around

the moon. Then I'll touch down . . . right beside you.

~ *Carmela A. Martino*

Mud Pies & Manatees

Ten more minutes! Not one more!
>   Why's my mother such a bore?

Can't she see I'm having fun?
Baking mud pies in the sun,
Digging tunnels, climbing trees,
Chasing after bumblebees.

Time to get into the tub!
>   Bath time? No way! What's to scrub?

Dusty elbows, dirty knees?
Hair with just a couple fleas?
Grubby cheeks, and crusty toes?
I like having all of those!

Get in now! I want you clean!
>   No more playtime? That's so mean!

Wait. There're bubbles? Then okay!
I could splash in here all day!
I'm a flipping dolphin! Wee!
Giant squid! A manatee!

Ten more minutes! Not one more!
>   Why's my mother such a bore?

>   ~ Aixa Perez-Prado

Extra Needed

Just ten more minutes,
please, Mom,
while Jeanie and I
play hide 'n seek.

Just ten more minutes,
please, Dad,
sing the last lines
again with me.

Just ten more minutes
please, Joe,
don't let me go
without a word.

Just ten more minutes
to say a prayer,
to give a hug,
to say you're there.

With all the hope
and all the care
to muster up
a smile
somewhere.

> ~ *Linda Baie*

I Couldn't Put It Down

My chores remained unfinished
The lawn wasn't mowed
Because I
Had to
Finish reading my book

My life's work halted
My grand plans went on hold
Because I
Had to
Finish reading my book

Large cities declined
Empires fell
Because I
Had to
Finish reading my book

Martians invaded
Zombies ran amok
Because I
Had to
Finish reading my book

~ Alan j Wright

*"**Tension** is who you think you should be. Relaxation is who you are."*

~ Chinese Proverb

The Greatest Show on Earth

One hundred feet above the crowd

with no net below

the tightrope walker extends her left leg

holds it

    just

        above

            the

                wire

while the crowd grows

silent as a midnight snow

Her foot finds rope

She shifts her weight

tests the tension

knows it

must be in the rope

in the crowd

but not in her

The people below

are in for a show

Up on the platform

she finds focus, exhales

becomes a spider

    precisely

        stepping

            on her own

                silk strand

Two

    four

      six

        steps

          across

the rope creaks

stretches

threatens to

SNAP!

She wobbles

Moans rush up at her from below

someone yells,

"NO!"

She stops

settles for a moment

becomes a bird

    on

        a

            slender

                twig

Moving again

    closer

        closer

          closer

the end

so near

she SLIPS!

Drops her pole!

The crowd SHRIEKS

CRIES

People cover their eyes

But LOOK!

She skims to the end

a water-strider on a mirrored pond

takes a bow toward the cheering crowd

and yawns

~ Marilyn Garcia

The Floating Water Strider

Skates on the pond;
it never sinks.

Water is helpful
to bugs when you think

how molecules huddle
together to float

the six legged strider
like a little bug boat.

~ *Janice Scully*

Counting Down...

Probing shadows of cold cruel night
imagination governs time
brings evil things that hang in space
above the bed, below the roof

always creaking, never speaking
plucking tight taut strands of fear
feathering threats of doom to come.

Beneath the sheets some haven calls -
can hiding work 'til morning wins

reprieve for he who shelters there?

~ *David Edge*

Her Fur Is Soft as Mittens, But . . .
(a poem of tens: can you find them all?)

I'd forgotten her needling teeth,
though they'd bitten me before.

And blood glistens
    from ten teeny tiny claws
      that extend and gouge
        my tender arm.
          Pay attention.

Listen. Learn.

Kittens are combat experts
camouflaged in cuteness!

~ Laura Purdie Salas

Why Raindrops Are Round

Water rains down
from clouds to the ground—
plump silver droplets
bounce all around,

each housed in shiny
watery skin,
keeping its treasure
tightly within.

            ~ Janice Scully

The Grammar Police

Anna Gram thought her teacher

Miss Anthrop

Was an undercover agent

-for the Grammar Police.

Anna feared for the words huddled in her notebook.

...maybe her nouns were common

Her verbs somewhat passive?

Did her adjectives demonstrate?

She knew some of her pronouns had trouble reaching agreement

-and her infinitives had split.

She suspected some of her ellipses may have been guilty of having an extra dot.

She occasionally misplaced her modifiers

And far too many of her sentences were simple and this gave her a complex.

She felt her vowels rumble and her colon collapse.

Her hopes had come to a full stop.

There, their, they're

Said her friend, Con Junction.

I will hide her red pen...

~ *Alan j Wright*

Releasing the Tension

Breathe in deep.

Close your eyes.

Pay attention

to the tension.

      Tightness in your forehead?

      Stiffness in your neck?

      Pressure in your chest?

Breathe out—long and slow,

from your head down to your toes.

Picture the stress

    floating

        up,

          up,

            up,

               and away,

    whispering,

"Good-bye,"

as

it

goes.

~ Carmela A. Martino

Tug of War

Heels dig in, teeth are bared, toes to temples taut

Dominate the middle - the goal that must be sought

Tension thrums tendons in each grippers' grasp

Champions cling to that rope with an iron clasp

Shoulders bunch, bent knees bow to Earth

The tuggers heave and ho!

The same song pounds in every heart

"Hang tight! Don't let go!"

An ancient competition where mind is met by might

The goal to win the battle is not just about the fight

Slackening the **ten**sion - knowing when to rest,

Is how this game of strength is played by those who play it best.

~ Moe Phillips

His Chair

His chair!

His chair lay in pieces.

That spiteful,

golden-tressed girl broke it.

Who did she think she was?

Waltzing in here,

scoffing his oatmeal,

snoozing in his bed?

It was his chair!

Not hers.

~ Angela De Groot

"Touch that with a 10-foot pole

I will not."

 ~ Yoda

Crocodile

I went to visit the River Nile,

whilst out upon a stroll.

Suddenly I saw a crocodile,

lying down near the watering hole.

It grinned at me and showed its teeth.

I wouldn't touch that with a 10-foot pole!

Lest its jaws close with me beneath

and gobbles me up whole.

~ Meenakshi Dwivedi

I Wouldn't Touch That With a Ten-Foot Pole

Snakes:
rattlers,
copperheads.
Also spiders:
black tarantulas,
goliath birdeaters.
In the ocean: great white sharks,
box jellyfish, barracudas.
On land: poison ivy, poison oak.
I'd touch NONE of them with a ten-foot pole.

~ Mary Lee Hahn

10 Things I Wouldn't Do

I wouldn't touch a tiger with a 10-foot pole.

I wouldn't nudge a narwhal with a 9-foot pole.

I wouldn't irk an ape with an 8-foot pole.

I wouldn't stroke a serpent with a 7-foot pole.

I wouldn't scrub a stingray with a 6-foot pole.

I wouldn't flick a falcon with a 5-foot pole.

I wouldn't flip a ferret with a 4-foot pole.

I wouldn't thwack a thistle with a 3-foot pole.

I wouldn't tease a T-Rex with a 2-foot pole.

I wouldn't whirl a weasel with a 1-foot pole.

Forget it. I won't do them. If you ask me, I'll oppose...

but I wouldn't miss a kitty kiss right on the nose.

~ Elizabeth Steinglass

At Your Disposal

It drives around the neighborhoods,
down lanes and gravel roads,
and stops wherever people need
to lighten heavy loads.

The folks all know it's coming through--
they signal invitation.
The youngsters often watch for it
with much anticipation.

No matter what they've bottled up,
it treats them all the same
by giving aid to everyone
and never calling shame.

With arms of steel, it lifts them up,
like each is but a feather
then lets them empty what's inside--
a cleansing done together.

It gently sets them back in place
much lighter than before,
and promises to come again
to rescue and restore.

~ Colleen Owen Murphy

A Smoother Frog

That's it.

No more waiting
for soft lips
to bestow a sticky
kiss against
my smooth, green skin
in hopes this curse
will speed away.

I'd rather spend
my days scraping
moss from these stones
and smashing flies
with my slap shot of saliva
than sit through another state
dinner where words poke and prod
like slower, stickier fingers.

No more perching
on a velvet pillow
behind a silken screen
in hopes this curse
will speed away.

I'd rather shoot

for the stars

as a smoother frog

than wait one more day

for a sticky kiss.

~ Kay Jernigan McGriff

Old King Cole's Secret

Old King Cole was a merry old soul
and a merry old soul was he.
But I wouldn't touch him with a ten-foot pole,
'cause he never could hold his pee.

Old King Cole was a pleasant old soul
and his laughter made his belly dance.
Oh, I wouldn't touch him with a ten-foot pole,
'cause he laughed until he wet his pants.

Old King Cole was a sorrowful soul,
and he sat up there all alone.
No, I wouldn't touch him with a ten-foot pole,
'cause he tinkled right on his throne.

Old King Cole was a pitiful soul
as he dribbled all over the rug.
I didn't want to touch him with a ten-foot pole,
but he pleaded: "Can you spare a hug?"

Old King Cole was a merry old soul

and he beamed at my running jump.

I sped and I leapt like a frisky foal,

so I'd hug him above his rump!

~ *Stephan Stuecklin*

Mud Café

Behind the old farmhouse, inside the tin shack,
lurks a diner you'll try—and then never come back.
You may note a strong smell that wafts straight to your
nose—
if you wander too close, it just might curl your toes!

You'll be welcomed most warmly to Faye's Mud Café,
though she'll lock the front door so you can't run away!
She may offer you coffee that's dripping with sludge,
or black tea whose consistency's firmer than fudge.

Her squishy brown pies are on special today,
or perhaps you'd prefer the chef's slimy soufflé?
Try sorbet laced with grass that gets stuck in your teeth;
at the bottom's a bonus—what's crawling beneath?

Why not sample her sauces—they're swimming in moss—
and the gravel-tossed salads cause certain tooth loss.
There are no foods to purchase that don't taste like crud;
that's because (what a shocker!) they're all full of mud.

A result of your visit to Faye's Mud Café
will be lingering odors: you'll stink like old hay!
One final matter may cause some dismay—
Faye's policy: "Customers MUST all prepay!"

~ *Jennifer Raudenbush*

I Would Not or Maybe I Would

I would not touch that with a ten foot pole.

I would not jump into a deep deep hole.

I would not skip around the whole block.

I would not walk wearing one sock.

I would not run too fast.

I would not be last.

I would not trot.

I would not.

I would.

I

I would.

I would hop.

I would yell, "stop".

I would take a hike.

I would ride my red bike.

I would ring the bell, ding, ding.

I would push my sister on the swing.

I would flash dance to loud rock and roll.

I would sing songs around that tall ten foot pole.

~Kathleen Mazurowski

Reverie Day

Hmmm, I wonder what I'll do today?
Maybe I'll teach a buzzard ballet,

or run a relay with sprinting skinks,
and practice juggling friendly minks.

An elephant could teach me to paint--
unless the mess made my parents faint.

Though I'll ride the spray from a whale's blowhole,
I won't touch a snake with a ten-foot pole.

A python just might give me a squeeze-
I would feel safer playing with bees!

Mornings are great for dreaming my day
and planning my stunt girl resume.

~ Tabatha Yeatts

"ten little fingers
ten little toes
two little eyes
one little nose"

~ Unknown

Finger Counting Rhyme

One, two,
we're going to the zoo.

Three, four,
lions roar.

Five, six,
anteater licks.

Seven, eight,
sloths sleep late.

Nine, ten,
count again.

~ Linda Mitchell

New mom kisses count

Ten little fingers, ten little toes

Smiles crease two faces

~ David Edge

Tenderness Times Ten

Ten tiny fingers, ten tiny toes,
Ten little frecklets sprinkled on your nose.
Ten gurgly giggles, ten toothless grins
Joy spills everywhere when I chuck your chin.
Ten stars wandering through the darkening sky
Fell from the heavens right into your eyes.
Ten dancing angels carried you to earth
While ten joyful moonbeams sang for your birth
You, my darling, have filled my cup again,
And so I give you tenderness times ten.

~ Susan Bruck

Ten Little Fingers

Ten little fingers to press
the eighty-eight black and white keys.
Ten little fingers to dress
in gloves when it's zero degrees.

Ten little fingers to scratch
the itch on the tip of your nose.
Ten little fingers to match
a finger for each of your toes.

Ten little fingers to click
a hurry let's go kind of beat.
Ten little fingers to flick
beach sand that sticks to your feet.

Ten little fingers to cross
in hope when you're feeling unsure.
Ten little fingers in gloss,
shellac or a French manicure.

Ten little fingers to count
but ten is as high as it goes,
so when all the fingers run out
add in your ten little toes!

~ Elenore Byrne

Otter

Otter climbs up the river bank—
ten toes in front, ten toes in back.
Otter scoots down the muddy slope,
on her slippy-slidey track.

Otter glides in the rippling brook,
grabs a tasty crayfish snack.
Otter rolls to the river bank—
chomps her lunch -- *crack, crack, crack.*

Otter runs on the river bank—
stops at the slippy-slidey track.
One more scoot down the muddy slope,
ten toes in front, ten toes in back.

~ *Buffy Silverman*

Ten Fingers, One Piano

Soaring,

                    sliding,

          flitting,

                        gliding.

Fingers dance across the keys,

playing with a gentle ease.

        Tapping,

                    trilling,

             skipping,

  thrilling,

'til the crowd cheers "Encore, please!"

                    ~ Susan Johnston Taylor

To Ten...And Then Again

A boy of five, he counts his sheep,
And counts to number ten.
He wants to play, he battles sleep,
And so begins again.

A boy of five, he counts his toes,
And counts to number ten.
He wants to play, his giggling grows,
And so begins again.

A boy of five, he finger-counts,
And counts to number ten.
His eyes they blink, the weary mounts,
But he begins again.

A boy of five, he counts his Dad.
And only counts to one.
His eyes they droop, is sleep so bad?

"Good night to you, my son."
                    ~ Dave Goodale

Hand Prints

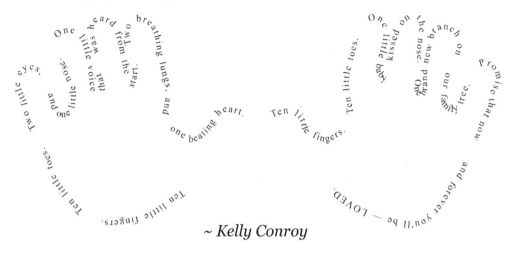

One little eyes, Two little owl and one little nose. One heard a owl was that little voice from the start. breathing lungs, and one beating heart. Ten little fingers. Ten little fingers. Ten little toes.

One little baby kissed on the nose. One Grand new branch on our family tree. Ten little toes. Promise that now and forever you'll be — LOVED.

~ Kelly Conroy

Celebrating Baby's Digits

ten little fingers, ten little toes
wiggle
giggle
touch
nose
wiggle
tickle
dance
pose
with
ten little fingers, ten little toes
~ Carol Varsalona

77

*"Sometimes you have to take two steps back to **take ten** forward."*

~ Nipsey Hussle

Kitchen Band

Clatter! Bang! Crash! Whack! Bop!

Mama sings, "A' doo, wop, wop."

 I strike pots with wooden spoons

Sister twirls, she loves these tunes.

Mama says, "Let's all take ten,

Have a snack, then play again!"

~ *Cathy Chester*

Keeping the Peace

I sit on my hands.
Bite back the urge.
Take a deep breath,
and meditate.
"The high road," I whisper.
"Ten, nine, eight . . ."
Breathe peace out.

~ *Angela De Groot*

Respite

Where can I go?
    To escape the drama
    Walls closing in
    Relentless negative chatter
    My self-doubt.

The ocean tempts me
    Urging my approach
    A gentle breeze, the salty scent
    Cool water envelops my toes
    Waves rhythmically lapping the beach
    Tasting the spray on my lips.

The sun warms me, my muscles relax.
    I've exited my head, breathing deeply
    Grateful to be alive.
    Words a memory, no longer heard.

The sea
        Relieves me
        Refreshes me
        Restores me
        Revives me

God whispers

Rest and take ten.

~ Helen Magee

Take 10 to Find Ten

Skipping in sunshine
puffy clouds overhead,
we flop on the grass,
it's our cloud-watching bed.

We angle our heads
look way up high,
play a game called Find Ten
as the shapes float by.

I spy a tiger,
a bear, then a pig
who looks oh so happy
cause she's dancing a jig!

We see a spaceship
headed straight out of sight,
trailing bright plumes of
vapor, foamy and bright.

Next there's a dragon
who's not breathing fire.
He's chasing three fish.
Yikes! Their future looks dire!

We squint at the sky
what else do we see?
There's a sweet little car
and a tiny pony!

It's time for our lunch,
yet there's still more to find
in our fluffy sky-sea
filled with shapes of all kinds!

~ Janet Fagal

Counting on Mistakes

One, two,

what did I do?

Three, four

Can I sink through the floor?

Five, six,

What's the fix?

Seven, eight,

It's not too late.

Nine, ten,

I'll try again.

~ Kay Jernigan McGriff

Sea Glass Searching

I love to search for sea glass

along the beach shoreline.

Colored shimmers in the sand

washed up by foamy brine.

Chunks of white and specks of green,

some bits of red and blue.

Trash from many years ago

the waves have made brand new.

Ten tiny, shiny treasures

now rest safe in my hand.

A present from the ocean

for my garden fairyland!

~ Shanah Salter

Ten Ghosts

Take ten ghosts on Halloween.

Nine were scary and looked so mean.

Eight were noisily clinking chains.

Seven were covered in ghostly stains.

Six were busy rattling door handles.

Five were trying to blow out the candles.

Four sat relaxing in comfy seats.

Three were trying to gobble up sweets.

Two were howling and started to weep.

While one just wanted to go back to sleep!

~ *Meenakshi Dwivedi*

*"Wizard's **Tenth** Rule Willfully turning aside from the truth is treason to one's self."*
~ Terry Goodkind

My Tenth Birthday

I'm ten today. I feel much more
grown-up than I did before.
I'm double digits. Taller too.
And there are new things I can do:
Use the oven. I can bake
cookies, brownies, chocolate cake.
Get my ears pierced. Ride my bike
as far as Merriweather Pike.
Attend my cousin's baby shower.
Stay up later by an hour.
I got a brand new sparkly phone.
And a bank account – my very own.
Teenager? Three years to go.
For now it's cheers –
the big ONE-O!

~ Eileen Spinelli

Tenth of an Inch

There once was a tenth of an inch.
A measurement only good in a pinch –
Like when sprinkling salt
Or unlocking a vault.
Any other uses make me flinch.

~ Maureen Magee-Uhlik

Winning at Tenth

I
came in
tenth place when
I entered that
contest at my school.
Some might say that I lost.
Not me. I was terrified
but I saw it through to the end.
I shook the fear, took the risk, and won:
I let them read my poetry out loud.

~ Karen Edmisten

Tenth Month

maples
trade green
for gold,

treasure
drops
   f l o a t s—

a shipwreck
for chipmunks
and children

to plunder
as ravens
announce

to one and all:
October!
   October!

                    ~ Irene Latham

the amber light of the sun

my gran
was born in the tenth month
perhaps that's why it it's
my favorite
because she is the golden hymn
that sews me together on the darkest days
she is the yellow butterfly and the yellow rose,
and the amber light of the sun;
warmth and radiance and support
have always wrapped their arms around me
even when no one believed in me

she did
even when others told me to abandon my dreams
she stood by my side,
telling me to keep my dreams.

~ linda m. crate

Tenth Text Says It All

My text to you:
misunderstood.

Our conversation
wasn't good.

To you, my motive
seemed unkind

To me, your judginess
seemed blind.

I'm trying to connect
with you.

It's such a tricky thing
to do.

You used to read
with understanding.

My words would find
a happy landing.

But now you turn my
thoughts away.

Oh well. There's nothing left
to say.

~ *Ruth Bowen Hersey*

The Jaunty Letter J

Behind I
but before K,
resides the jaunty letter J.

Tenth letter in the alphabet,
but first in jumbo,
jumble,
and jovial.

Whether she feels uppercased -
standing tall and
wearing a horizontal hat
or lowercased –
dipping below the line
donning her dainty dot,
J always swoops left.

J is soft spoken,
jazzy and jolly,
but can sometimes be mistaken for
the soft pronunciation of G –
giraffe, much?

When abroad

 J has even been known

to sound like Y!

She doesn't know why.

While she does start junk

judgement,

and jealousy,

she is also a juggernaut

for some of the most popular

baby names *ever*:

James

Jennifer

John

and Jessica.

Keep J in mind

when you need

a jolt

a joke

or justice.

And remember,

without J

joy is reduced

to *oy* -

no one wants

to hear that!

> ~ *Bridget Magee*

"I tend to watch silently from the shadows. You learn a lot more that way."

~ Sherrilyn Kenyon

Tend With Wonder

Tend the garden.
Wet the bed.
Twist the weeds and pull.

Tendrils tip
With promises
Frilly, fine, and full.

Tend the harvest.
Snap the peas.
Call upon the guests.

Tend the feeders.
Watch the birds.
When the garden rests.

~ Marty Lapointe-Malchik

TLC

I tend to my garden.
I tend to my fish.
I tend to my heart
with each quiet wish.

Things tend to get busy.
Things tend to get tough.
I tend to my soul;
then there's enough

of me
to tend to you, too!

~ Robyn Hood Black

A Professional Riddle

I tend to

Puppy paws and kitten claws

Birds with beaks and mice who squeak

Guinea pigs and rabbits, too.

Who am I? What do I do?

answer: veterinarian

~ Elisabeth Norton

Quitting

I tend to give up
when a problem or task
or a game or a race is too rough.
I call it a day.
I throw in the towel.
I quit when the going gets tough.

I'd rather not finish
than not finish first.
I try never to say 'lose' out loud.
But I'm often alone
while friends finish their race
and I've noticed I rarely feel proud.

It is weird they run on
even after they know
that they probably will not be first.
But they never give up
even when they're behind.
They don't seem like they think it's the worst.

They are glad when they win,
not too sad when they lose.
Kinda wish I was them and so I
think that when things get tough
I won't stop, I won't quit.
I will gather my courage and try.

~ Rebekah Hoeft

Weathered Tendencies

I have this tendency to be nervous
when a storm is coming.

Weather people have a tendency
to speak with the facts
(along with the hope)
that this storm
will break records.

The tenth time they broadcast,
I Google how to turn off my water
in case the pipes freeze.

~ Linda Baie

Talking to Hear Myself Speak

I tend to jibber.
I tend to jabber.
Alone or together,
I tend to blabber.

I tend to chitter.
I tend to chatter.
About what?
It doesn't matter.

~ Bridget Magee

through the years

i tend to think of you
on gray days
because they remind me
of your eyes

i remember them as gray,
but in gran's picture
they're blue;

i remember it was raining
on the day of the funeral
and my cousin scolded me for
crying over someone we didn't know—

but i wrote you letters,
and i loved you;
i don't think grief is something
anyone should be scolded for
yet he was so bold as to say i didn't
know you

but you were my uncle and you wrote
me letters and i wished one day
you could've taught me to paint—

it's been twenty years since you left us,
and i've thought a lot about you
through the years.
                    ~ *linda m. crate*

I'm Sorry

Sometimes when I'm angry,

I tend to say things

I really don't mean
and hurt someone I love.

Then I sit alone
wishing I could take
back my prickling words.

But—
I don't know what to say
to make things right again.

So I stay silent.

Too mad.
Too sad.
To say,
I'm sorry.

~ Linda Kulp Trout

What Tends to Happen

Spring again
Hoe in hand

I work the soil
Earthworms roil

Pull the weeds
Plant some seeds

Water deep
Plan to reap

But then ...

Days get warm
Insects swarm

New weeds grow
I stub my toe

Mud stains
Interest wanes

Woodchucks excavate
Grubs decimate

Caterpillars chew
I'm through

Plants wilt
I gather guilt

End of tale...
Epic fail!

So...

Next spring's plan...
Try again?

Or... alas...
more grass?

~ *Karen Eastlund*

Who Wrote What

LINDA BAIE

Linda Baie is a retired teacher and literacy coach from Denver, Colorado. Passions are grandchildren, reading, writing and being outdoors. In these retirement years, she is serving as the volunteer coordinator of a used bookstore run only by volunteers. It's a wonder of a place to be.

MICHELLE HEIDENRICH BARNES

Michelle Heidenrich Barnes is a children's poet and anthologist from Florida. A finalist for Alachua County Poet Laureate, she has poems in several anthologies, including A WORLD FULL OF POEMS, I AM SOMEONE ELSE, THE POETRY OF US, and ONE MINUTE TILL BEDTIME. For more information, visit www.MichelleHBarnes.com.

ROBYN HOOD BLACK

Robyn Hood Black is a poet, children's author, and artist hailing from both sides of South Carolina – the Lowcountry and the Upstate. Her work appears in numerous anthologies, magazines, and leading haiku journals. She also creates literary art and gifts through her Etsy business, artsyletters®.

JAY BRAZEAU

Jay Brazeau is an emerging poet who once won a hamburger for a poem about chicken. He resides in Ottawa, Canada but lives on the outer edge of imagination. His ten more minutes on a roller coaster passed...slowly.

SUSAN BRUCK

Susan Bruck is a poet, artist, teacher, and handworker. She has spent many years working with little ones--who always inspire her and remind her of what's important in life. She's the mom of two grown-up daughters and currently plays and works in sunny Colorado.

ELENORE BYRNE

Elenore Byrne lives in Switzerland with her husband and 3 children. Before this, she worked with kids as a Clinical Psychologist in New Zealand. When she is not writing she is trying to keep up with her busy family. You can visit her online at elenorewrites.wordpress.com.

CATHY CHESTER

After teaching Math and Science in Middle School for 42 years, Cathy Chester returned to her love of writing. Inspired by two generations of nieces' and nephews' wordplay, she loves to dabble in the rhymes and rhythms of their everyday lives. Take the time to listen to little ones, incredibly fun.

KELLY CONROY

When she's not creating picture books, poems, or prints, Kelly Conroy loves going on adventures, playing games, and chatting around a campfire. She lives in Western Pennsylvania with her husband, two fun sons, and mini goldendoodle, Chewy.

LINDA M. CRATE

Linda M. Crate's works have been published in numerous magazines and anthologies. She is the author of seven poetry chapbooks, the latest of which is: *the samurai* (Yellow Arrow Publishing, October 2020). She has also authored three micro-collections, and four full length poetry collections.

MARY E. CRONIN

Mary E. Cronin's poetry has appeared in *The New York Times*, in *Rhyme & Rhythm: Poems for Student Athletes*, in *Bronx Writers Anthology vol. 2*, and in the anthology *Amazing Faces* by Lee Bennett Hopkins. Mary has an MFA in Writing for Children and Young Adults from Vermont College of Fine Arts. Twitter @maryecronin

ANGELA DE GROOT

Angela De Groot was born in England, grew up in South Africa, and currently lives in New Jersey with her husband and sons. Angela's stories and poems have appeared in *Skipping Stones Magazine*, *The Edison Review*, and *Alive Now*. Angela hopes to make readers laugh and spark joy in reading.

MEENAKSHI DWIVEDI

Meenakshi Dwivedi is a doctor by profession and lives in the U.K. She is married to a doctor as well and finds her job incredibly rewarding. She enjoys spending time with her two children and going for long walks with her dog. She started writing during the pandemic and has found it enjoyable.

KAREN EASTLUND

Karen Eastlund reads for truth and writes for fun. The very process of writing, beginning in preschool, fascinates and inspires her. Karen pursues poetry for its rhythm and surprise, and has published in *The Saturday Evening Post* and *The Best of Today's Little Ditty 2016* and *2017-2018*. https://kceastlund.blogspot.com/

DAVID EDGE

David Edge was born an Englishman, retired a Californian, worked for the government in between. Occasionally (still) indulges in dietary and poetic excess.

KAREN EDMISTEN

Karen Edmisten is a freelance writer, poet, the author of five books, and a writing coach who delights in helping young writers find their voices. Find her online at karenedmisten.com.

JANET FAGAL

Retired teacher and poet Janet Fagal, known for her poetry advocacy and work with children, celebrates poetry's beauty and power through enthusiasm, recitation, performance, and composing. Her poems appear in Pomelo Books' anthologies as well as Lee Bennett Hopkins' 2019 I AM SOMEONE ELSE. Also online at nlapw.org. jfagal@gmail.com

DANIEL J. FLORE III

Daniel J. Flore III's poems have appeared in many publications. He is the author of 4 books of poetry from GenZ Publishing.

MARILYN GARCIA

Marilyn Garcia is a writer and reading mentor living in Columbia, Maryland. She writes fiction and non-fiction for young readers, and poetry for all ages. You can find more of her work in *Hop To It: Poems to Get You Moving,* Pomelo Books, 2020.

DAVE GOODALE

Dave Goodale enjoys writing poetry for adults and children and is a member of the Society of Children's Book Writers and Illustrators. He also likes reading, watching football and soccer, studying the German language, and pecking at the piano. He pursues his writing dreams from his home in Connecticut.

MARY LEE HAHN

Mary Lee Hahn currently works at finding the best words for her poems, the best books to share on the blog, the best colors and lines for paper, and the best ways to serve her community.

RUTH BOWEN HERSEY

Ruth Bowen Hersey is an American who lives with her husband in Port-au-Prince, Haiti, where she teaches at an international school. Her children, both born in Haiti, are grown up, and she's figuring out the next stage of her life. She loves reading, writing, and birding.

CORINNE HERTEL

Corinne is a school librarian, fledgling poet, and transplanted Canadian who lives in a mountain village in Switzerland. She is honoured to have a piece selected for this anthology.

REBEKAH HOEFT

Rebekah Hoeft lives in Michigan with her husband and two children. She is a teacher at a Lutheran school in the metro Detroit area and loves to write and read.

MOLLY HOGAN

Molly Hogan is a fourth grade teacher who lives with her husband in an old Maine farmhouse. She spends her free time writing, gardening, wandering, and taking pictures. Much to her delight, she's had a smattering of personal essays and poems published, and had a gallery show of her photographs.

MICHELLE KOGAN

Michelle Kogan's writing and art grow from nature and humanity. She's in *Silver Birch Press' Prime Mover* series; and these poetry anthologies: *The Best of Today's Little Ditty volume I – III*, and *Imperfect: poems about mistakes: an anthology for middle schoolers*. Her artworks in collections and publications.
www.michellekogan.com
www.moreart4all.wordpress.com
www.MichelleKoganFineArt.etsy.com

MARTY LAPOINTE-MALCHIK

Marty Lapointe-Malchik is an educator, author, and illustrator featured in *An Assortment of Animals: A Children's Poetry Anthology, Friends and Anemones: Ocean Poems for Children, Highlights* and *High Five*. Trained in speech pathology and deaf education, Marty currently uses her passion for language teaching as an early intervention provider.

IRENE LATHAM

Irene Latham is a grateful creator of many novels, poetry collections, and picture books, including the coauthored *Can I Touch Your Hair?: Poems of Race, Mistakes, and Friendship*, which earned a Charlotte Huck Honor, and *The Cat Man of Aleppo*, which won a Caldecott Honor. Irene lives on a lake in rural Alabama.

BRIDGET MAGEE

Bridget Magee is an American expat who writes, teaches, and lives in central Switzerland where she is continually finding her voice, both in English and rudimentary German.

HELEN MAGEE

Helen Magee calmly dispatched emergency 9-1-1 calls, coached aqua aerobics at a community college, served as a church secretary, sold AVON products, taught others to write their life story and ushered at the Performing Arts Center. These varied vocations led her to write her memoir in retirement near the beach.

MAUREEN MAGEE-UHLIK

Maureen Magee-Uhlik doesn't usually write poetry. She spends most of her time reading, attending school, hanging out with her dog, and parenting her two fish.

CARMELA A. MARTINO

Carmela A. Martino is a writing teacher with an MFA in Writing for Children and Young Adults. She is the author of two award-winning novels: *Rosa, Sola* (Candlewick Press) and *Playing by Heart* (Vinspire Publishing). Carmela's articles, short stories, and poems have been published in newspapers, magazines, and anthologies. For more, see www.carmelamartino.com.

KATHLEEN MAZUROWSKI

Kathleen Mazurowski, retired elementary school teacher, is a regular at the Chicago Public Library. Her world travel plans paused, for now, she spends time reading, writing, and revising poems.

KAY JERNIGAN MCGRIFF

Kay Jernigan McGriff lives in Popcorn, IN, with her husband and occasional visits from her daughter. She has used her English degrees in a variety of ways from mission volunteer to middle school English teacher, freelance writer, and project manager. She loves to explore in books and travel.

CHRISTY MIHALY

Christy Mihaly is a children's poet and author. Her picture books include *Barefoot Books Water: A Deep Dive of Discovery; Free for You and Me;* and *Hey, Hey, Hay!* She lives near a Vermont pond and enjoys walking her dog and playing cello (though not simultaneously). Visit her at www.christymihaly.com.

LINDA MITCHELL

Linda Mitchell is a family girl, Teacher Librarian at a public middle school, and writes poems when she can get a word in Edgewise (also the name of her weekly poetry blog). She's thrilled to be included in this anthology.

COLLEEN OWEN MURPHY

Colleen Owen Murphy has been writing poetry since aged five. She's a pre-published author and the mother of three nearly-perfect daughters. Recently retired from teaching middle school math and English, much of her inspiration now comes from exploring and experiencing the environs of western Florida with her grandsons Owen and Jayden.

ELISABETH NORTON

Originally from the US, Elisabeth now lives in Switzerland, where she teaches English as a Foreign Language at a Swiss technical school. She writes picture books, chapter books and middle grade novels and serves as the Assistant International Advisor for Outreach for the Society of Children's Book Writers & Illustrators.

AIXA PEREZ-PRADO

Aixa Pérez-Prado is a Latinx writer, illustrator, translator and university professor. She has published two books on teaching, and created the cover art for both. Her passion is writing and illustrating books for children that celebrate diversity with heart and humor.
Website: aixaperezprado.com
Twitter: @professoraixa
Instagram: aixasdoodlesandbooks
TikTok: aixasdoodlesandbooks

LISA VARCHOL PERRON

Lisa Varchol Perron writes children's poetry, picture books, and middle grade novels. Her publication credits include *Highlights Hello*, *The Caterpillar*, and *The School Magazine*, and Lisa earned second place in the 2021 *Madness! Poetry* tournament for children's poets. She lives with her family just outside of Boston, Massachusetts.

MOE PHILLIPS

Poet/writer/ filmmaker Moe Phillips has been published in numerous anthologies for children and adults. Seven of her inspirational pieces have been featured in *Bella Grace Magazine*. Moe's latest creation is "The Feisty Beast". An audio content series she pens and produces. The elements and elementals are Moe's inspiration.

JENNIFER RAUDENBUSH

Jennifer Raudenbush feels most alive when she's creating stories, especially picture books and middle grade novels. Jen lives with her husband and son in eastern Pennsylvania, where natural beauty provides endless inspiration. She loves to cuddle with her pup and adventure with family. Connect with her: jenraudenbush.com or (Twitter) @jenraudenbush

LAURA PURDIE SALAS

Minnesota author Laura Purdie Salas has written more than 130 books, including *Lion of the Sky*, *Clover Kitty Goes to Kittygarten*, and *Snowman-Cold=Puddle*. Laura loves nature, donuts, and playing with words. She also loves to teach writers, write with teachers, and get kids excited about reading and writing. laurasalas.com

SHANAH SALTER

Shanah Salter started her career as a Family Physician in Australia. She now lives in Chicago with her family. When she's not being examined by the two mini-me's in her life, Shanah sneaks alone time to craft children's poetry and fiction, and review books.

JANICE SCULLY

Janice Scully lives in Upstate, New York, and is an MFA graduate of Vermont College and writes fiction and poetry for kids. Her work was published in Miranda Paul's 2019 anthology THANKU: POEMS OF GRATITUDE, and in Highlights for Children. She is also a physician and enjoys reading and writing non-fiction.

LAURA SHOVAN

Laura Shovan is the author of the award-winning middle grade novel-in-verse, *The Last Fifth Grade of Emerson Elementary*, and *Takedown*, a Junior Library Guild and PJ Our Way selection. *A Place at the Table*, co-written with Saadia Faruqi, is 2021 Sydney Taylor Notable. Laura is a longtime poet-in-the-schools in Maryland.

BUFFY SILVERMAN

Buffy Silverman writes nonfiction books for children, featuring topics from Angel Sharks to Alligators. Her most recent title, *On a Snow-Melting Day: Seeking Signs of Spring*, was an NCTE 2021 Notable Poetry Book. Look for her nature-inspired poetry in anthologies and children's magazines, and visit her at www.buffysilverman.com

DONNA JT SMITH

Donna JT Smith is retired from teaching and is revived with writing. She has had poems published in a number of anthologies. She lives in Maine in a little yellow house by the sea with her husband and little dog, Daisy. A Miss Rumphius wanna-be, Donna is almost there.

EILEEN SPINELLI

Eileen Spinelli began writing poetry when she was six years old. Her first poem was about a sailboat. When she is not writing or hanging out with family and friends she is reading, tending her herb garden, watching old movies, watching the birds in her backyard and browsing in thrift shops.

ELIZABETH STEINGLASS

Elizabeth Steinglass is that author of *Soccerverse: Poems about Soccer*, which includes 22 poems about all aspects of the game. You can also find her work in many anthologies, such as *A World Full of Poems*, edited by Sylvia Vardell and *The Poetry of US*, edited by J. Patrick Lewis.

STEPHAN STUECKLIN

Stephan Stuecklin writes picture books. Some of them rhyme. His self-published picture book "King Ron of the Triceratops" doesn't, except for its theme song. Stephan wrote that, too. He likes to write funny stuff, say, about pooping planets or dogs peeing. Stephan's day job is in a steel mill.

SUSAN JOHNSTON TAYLOR

Susan Johnston Taylor writes fiction, nonfiction, and poetry for curious kids. She's authored several historical fiction books for the educational market. Her STEM poetry collection, *Colorful Creatures: Poems About Animals in Surprising Shades,* will be published by Gnome Road Publishing in 2023. Learn more at www.susan-johnston.com.

LINDA J. THOMAS

Linda J. Thomas loves to capture the wonders of nature through writing and photography. Her poetry, essays, and photographs have appeared in several literary anthologies. Linda lives in New Hampshire with her husband and the birds, rabbits, deer, and occasional bear that visit their backyard. Her web address is lindajthomas.com.

LINDA KULP TROUT

Linda Kulp Trout's poems have appeared in multiple anthologies, textbooks, and magazines, and teacher resources. She retired after twenty-seven years teaching elementary and middle school and now writes books and poetry for children. She loves reading, writing, listening to music, spending time with her family, and walking in nature.

GERALDINE TYLER

Geraldine Tyler was born in County Down, Northern Ireland and grew up in the Irish countryside near the little, seaside village of Ballywalter. She immigrated to America when she was eighteen and currently lives in Arizona. She has a B.A. degree in English Literature from California State University, San Bernardino.

CAROL VARSALONA

Carol Varsalona is an English Language Arts consultant, writer/poet, blogger, certified wonderologist. She is the creator of online seasonal global galleries of artistic expressions focusing on poetry and photography to capture the beauty of nature and has published several poems in anthologies.

JANET WONG

Janet Wong (janetwong.com) is the recipient of the 2021 NCTE Excellence in Poetry for Children Award. Author of more than 35 books, including *A Suitcase of Seaweed & MORE*, she is the co-creator (with Sylvia Vardell) of *The Poetry Friday Anthology for Celebrations* and several other anthologies for classroom use.

ALAN j WRIGHT

Alan j Wright is an Australian poet and writer who has worked extensively in the US and throughout Australia in his capacity as an education consultant. He writes regularly on matters educational and has published three children's poetry anthologies to date.

TABATHA YEATTS

Tabatha Yeatts has edited and authored books for young adults, as well as written dozens of articles for magazines and newspapers and thousands of blog posts. She is busy figuring out new places to put plants and wishing she had an extra hand for petting her dogs while she writes.

Made in the USA
Middletown, DE
10 October 2021